PIANO *for* TWO

MW00595405

DUETS EQUAL PARTS FOR ONE PIANO, 4 HANDS

arranged by
Carol Matz

Production: Frank and Gail Hackinson
Production Coordination and Text Design: Marilyn Cole
Editors: Victoria McArthur and Edwin McLean
Cover: Terpstra Design, San Francisco
Engraving: GrayBear Music Company, Hollywood, Florida
Printer: Tempo Music Press, Inc.

THE
F·J·H
MUSIC
COMPANY
INC.

A Note to Teachers

Most students find duet playing to be a fun and challenging addition
to their everyday piano studies. Duets offer students a chance to
learn from the experience of making music with another person.
Piano for Two® provides a wonderful opportunity for students to work
on aspects of ensemble playing, such as dynamic balance and tempo
control, while learning some of their favorite well-known pieces.

The arrangements incorporate the use of eighth note and dotted-quarter
note rhythms. Circled finger numbers signal change of hand position.
Where needed, the pedal markings are indicated in the *secondo* part.

For easier reading, one or both parts call for an octave transposition,
which is clearly marked in the score. Additionally, the melodies often
shift between *primo* and *secondo,* affording the opportunity to work
on dynamic blending.

Piano for Two® is available in six volumes, ranging in difficulty from
early elementary through late intermediate/advanced levels. Students will
be delighted by the variety of pieces included in each book, representing
the classics, well-known favorites, original pieces, and more.

CONTENTS

Theme from
Eine Kleine Nachtmusik
Secondo

Wolfgang Amadeus Mozart

Quickly
(Play both hands 1 octave lower)

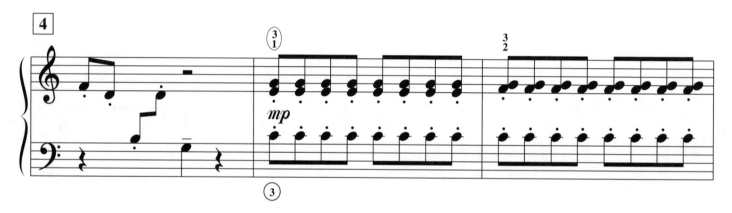

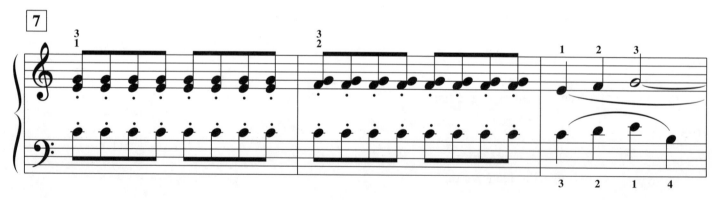

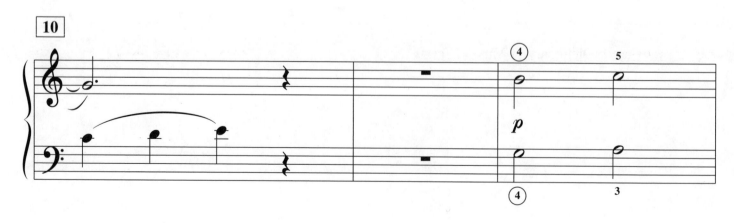

This arrangement © 1997 The FJH Music Company Inc.
International Copyright Secured.   Made in U.S.A.   All Rights Reserved.

Theme from
Eine Kleine Nachtmusik
Primo

Wolfgang Amadeus Mozart

Quickly
(Play both hands 1 octave higher)

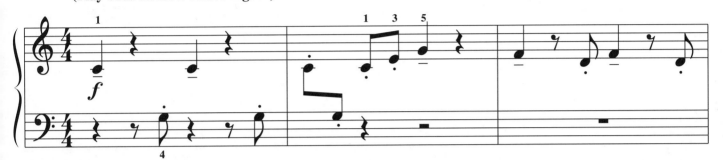

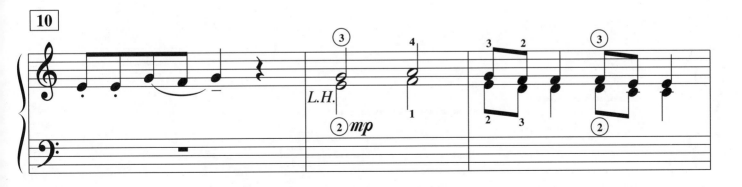

This arrangement © 1997 The FJH Music Company Inc.
International Copyright Secured.   Made in U.S.A.   All Rights Reserved.

Secondo

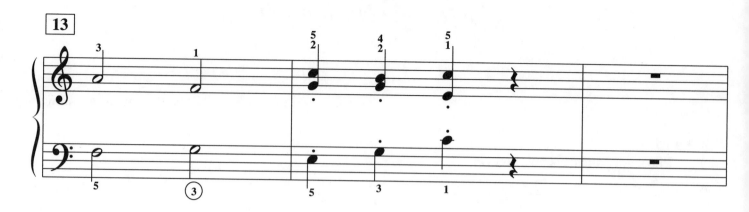

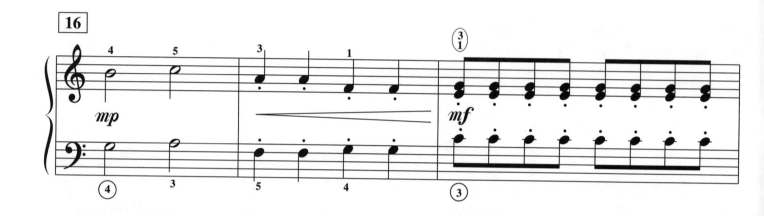

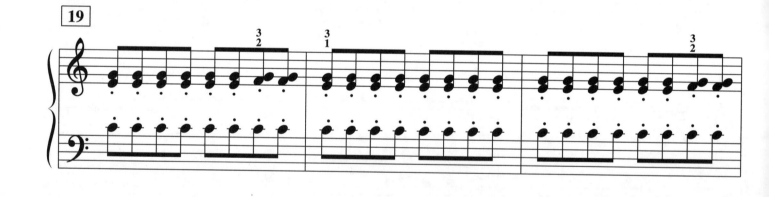

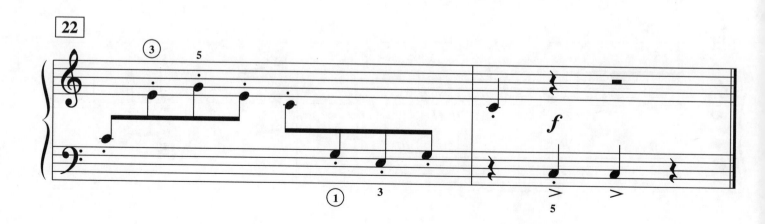

Primo

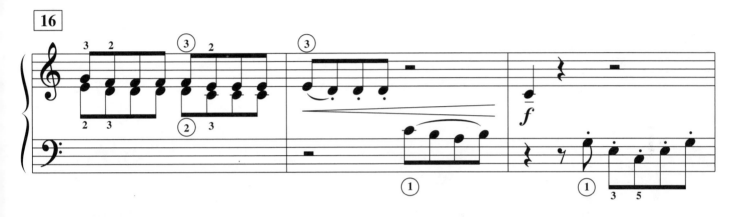

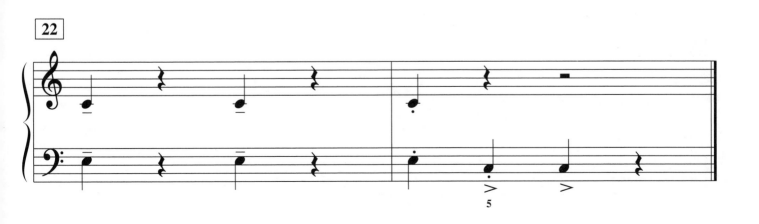

America the Beautiful

Secondo

Music by Samuel A. Ward
Words by Katherine Lee Bates

Flowing
(Play as written)

This arrangement © 1997 The FJH Music Company Inc.
International Copyright Secured.   Made in U.S.A.   All Rights Reserved.

America the Beautiful

Primo

Music by Samuel A. Ward
Words by Katherine Lee Bates

Flowing
(Play both hands 1 octave higher)

This arrangement © 1997 The FJH Music Company Inc.
International Copyright Secured.   Made in U.S.A.   All Rights Reserved.

FF1147

Secondo

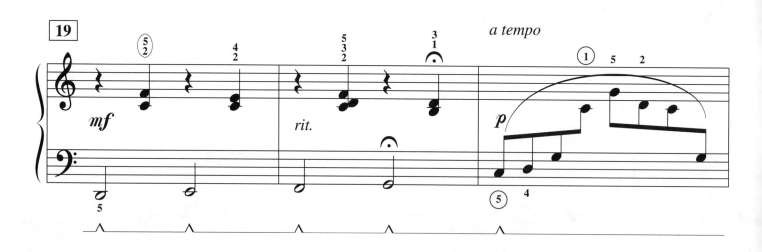

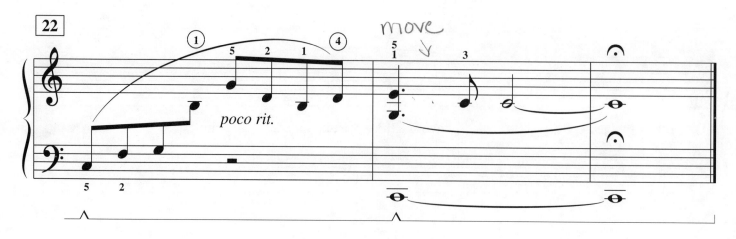

Sleeping Beauty Waltz

Secondo

Peter Ilyich Tchaikovsky

This arrangement © 1997 The FJH Music Company Inc.
International Copyright Secured.   Made in U.S.A.   All Rights Reserved.

Sleeping Beauty Waltz

Primo

Peter Ilyich Tchaikovsky

Moderate waltz
(Play both hands 1 octave higher)

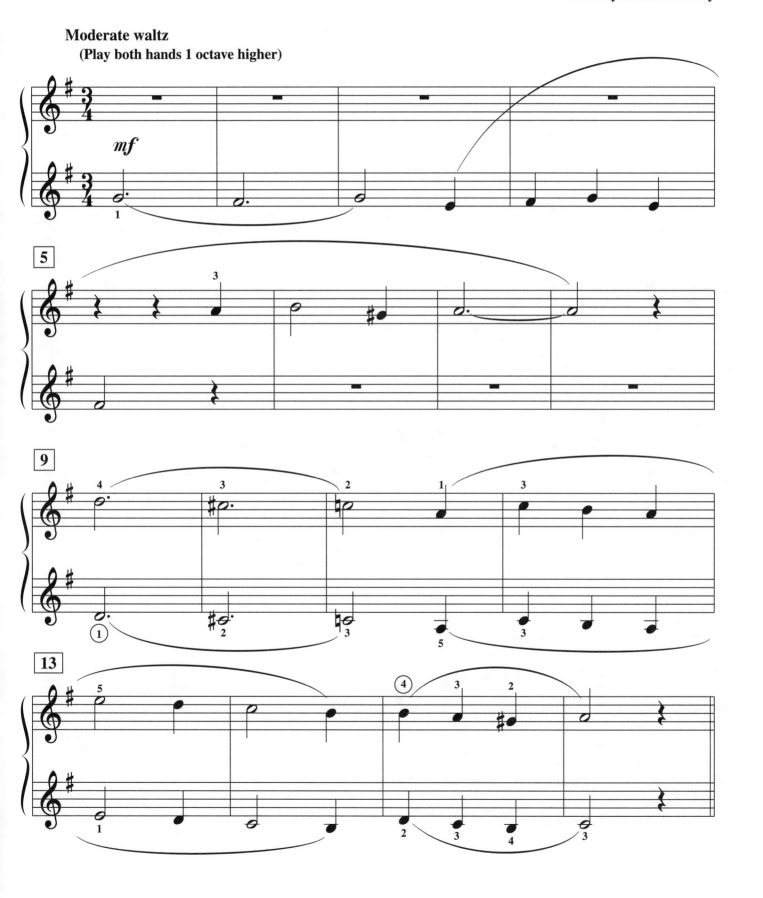

This arrangement © 1997 The FJH Music Company Inc.
International Copyright Secured.   Made in U.S.A.   All Rights Reserved.

Secondo

Primo

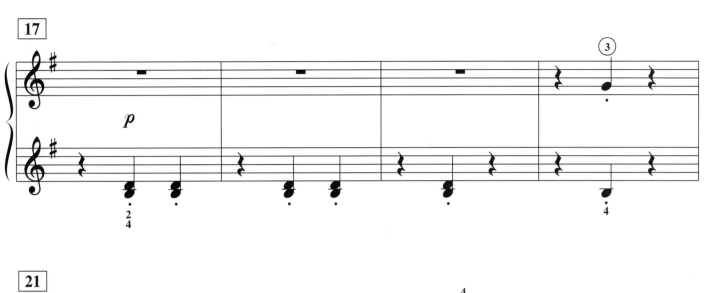

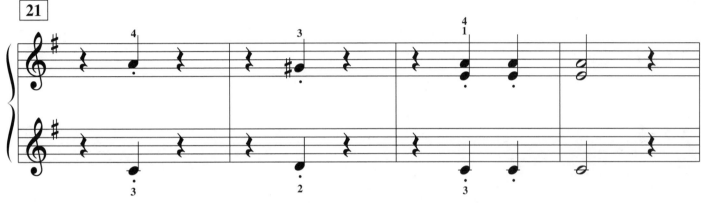

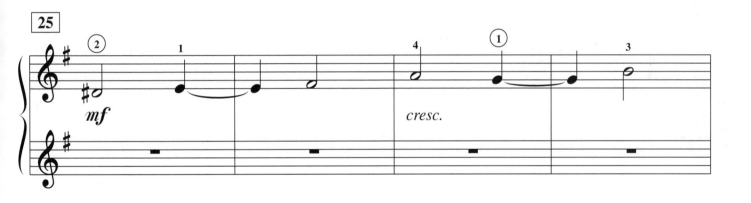

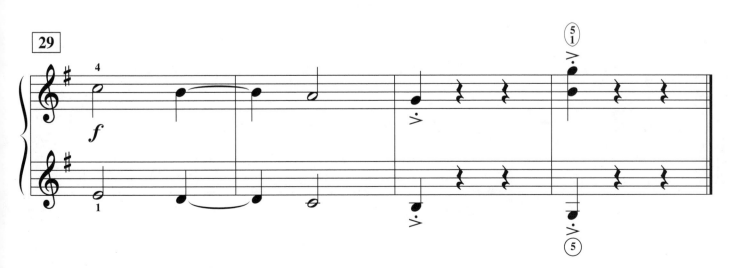

Main Street Rag

Secondo

Carol Matz

Copyright © 1997 The FJH Music Company Inc.
International Copyright Secured.   Made in U.S.A.   All Rights Reserved.

Main Street Rag

Primo

Carol Matz

Moderately fast
(Play both hands 1 octave higher)

Copyright © 1997 The FJH Music Company Inc.
International Copyright Secured.   Made in U.S.A.   All Rights Reserved.

FF1147

Secondo

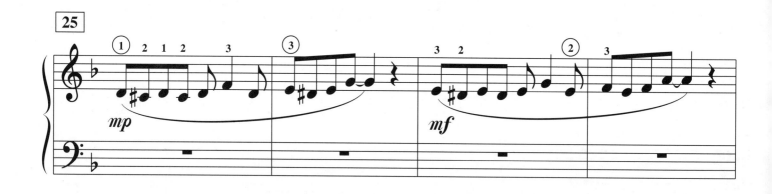

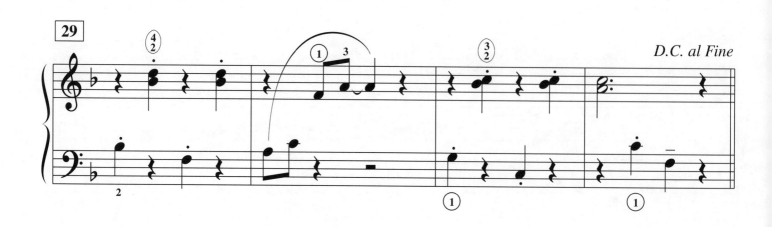

D.C. al Fine

Primo

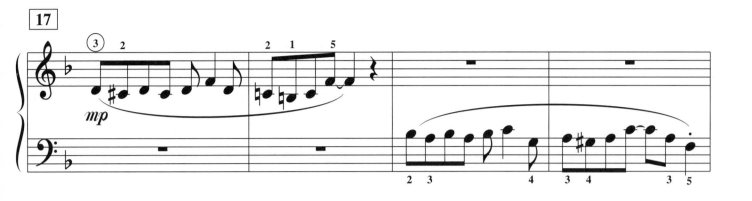

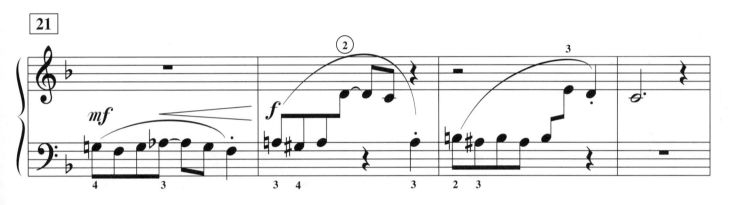

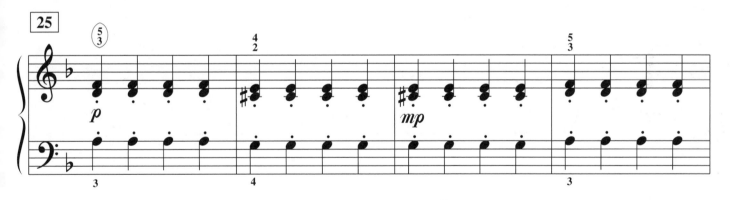

D.C. al Fine

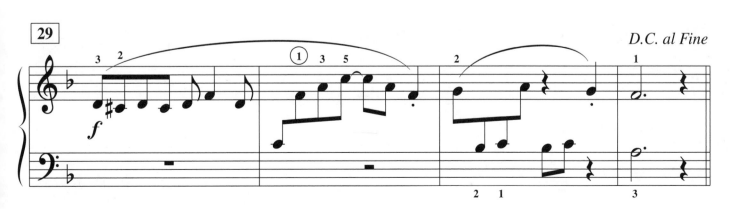

Swing Low, Sweet Chariot

Secondo

Traditional

This arrangement © 1997 The FJH Music Company Inc.
International Copyright Secured.   Made in U.S.A.   All Rights Reserved.

Swing Low, Sweet Chariot

Primo

Traditional

This arrangement © 1997 The FJH Music Company Inc.
International Copyright Secured.   Made in U.S.A.   All Rights Reserved.

Secondo

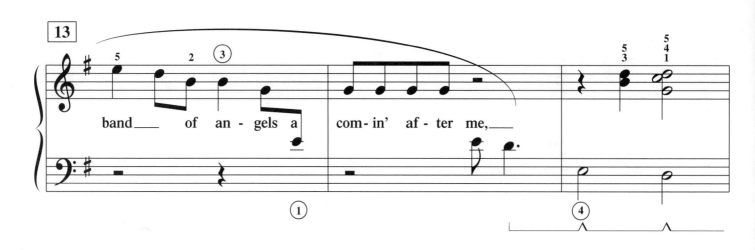

band_____ of an - gels a | com- in' af - ter me,_____

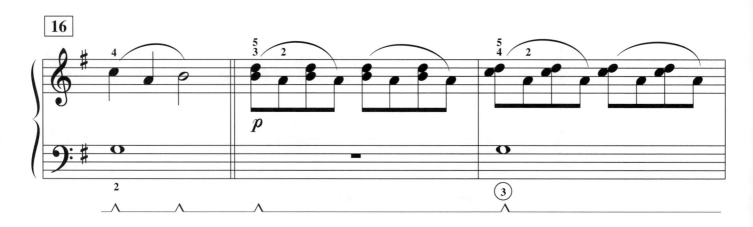

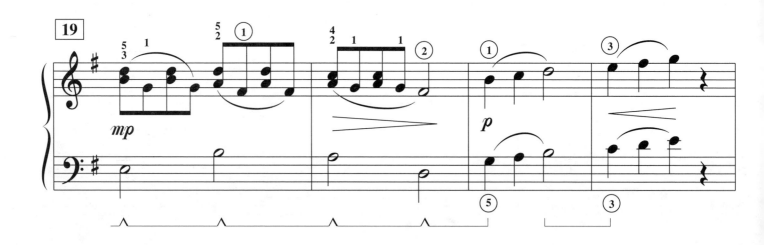

A little slower

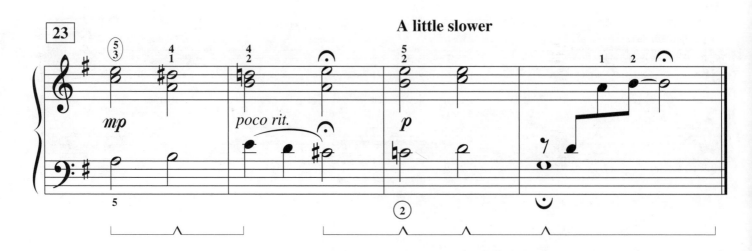

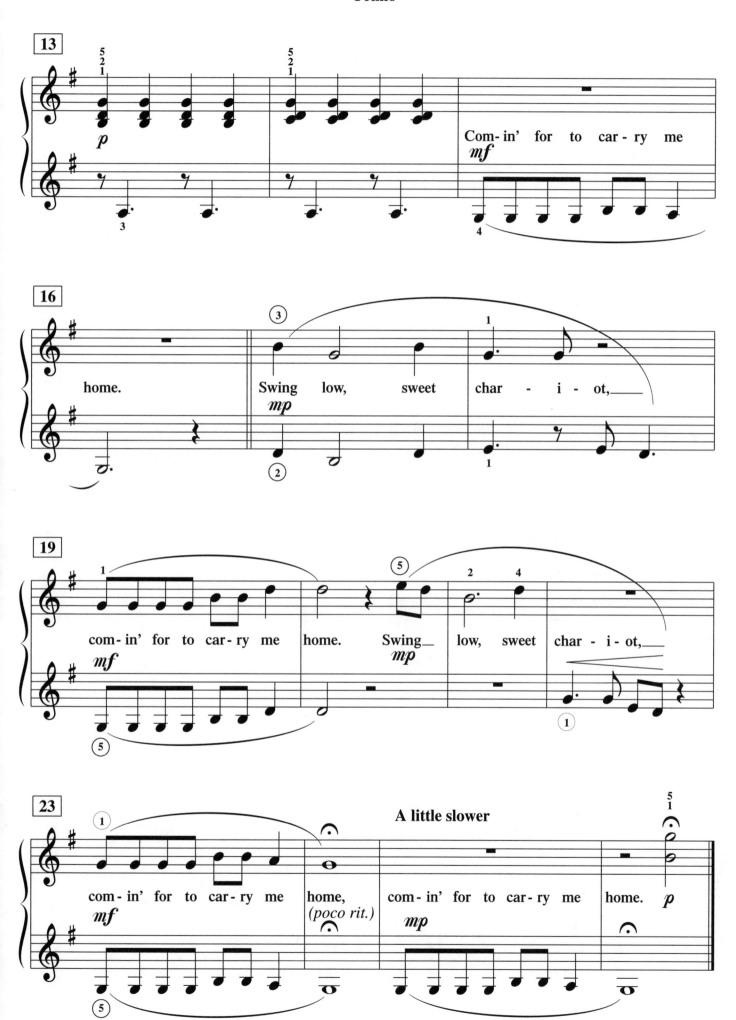

Hungarian Dance No. 5

Secondo

Johannes Brahms

This arrangement © 1997 The FJH Music Company Inc.
International Copyright Secured.   Made in U.S.A.   All Rights Reserved.

Hungarian Dance No. 5

Primo

Johannes Brahms

This arrangement © 1997 The FJH Music Company Inc.
International Copyright Secured.   Made in U.S.A.   All Rights Reserved.

FF1147

Secondo

Primo

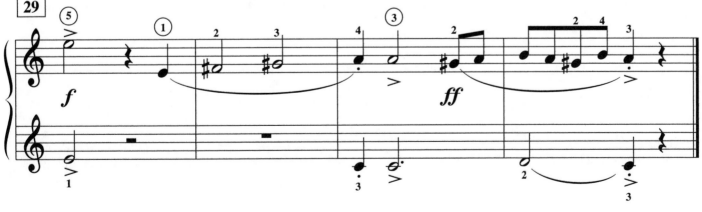

Dictionary of Musical Terms

staccato . . . . Play the note short and detached.

accent . . . . Play an accented note louder, with emphasis.

tenuto . . . . A slight stress. (Also known as a *stress mark.*)

slur . . . . Play these notes connected, smoothly.

rit.

ritardando . . . . Slow down gradually.

poco . . . . A little. (Ex.: *poco rit.* means a little or slight *ritardando.*)

fermata . . . . Hold the note longer than usual.

a tempo . . . . Return to the original speed.

octave . . . . A distance of 8 scale tones higher or lower.

pedal marking . . . . Depress and hold the damper pedal (right foot pedal). Lift at the end of the pedal marking.

pedal change . . . . Lift the pedal, then depress immediately.

8va

ottava . . . . When placed above a note or notes, play one octave higher than written. When placed below, play one octave lower.

D.C. al Fine . . . . *Da Capo al Fine.* Return to the beginning and play until the *Fine* (end).

Primo . . . . The first part in a duet. Refers to the music for the player sitting on the right.

Secondo . . . . The second part in a duet. Refers to the music for the player sitting on the left.

Dynamic Symbols

pp (*pianissimo*) . . . . .very soft

p (*piano*) . . . . .soft

mp (*mezzo-piano*) . . . . .medium soft

mf (*mezzo-forte*) . . . . .medium loud

f (*forte*) . . . . .loud

ff (*fortissimo*) . . . . .very loud

crescendo (*cresc.*)
play louder gradually

diminuendo (*dim.*)
play softer gradually